P9-CIW-126

# CLOTH LULLABY

## THE WOVEN LIFE OF LOUISE BOURGEOIS

WORDS BY
AMY NOVESKY

PICTURES BY
ISABELLE ARSENAULT

ABRAMS BOOKS FOR YOUNG READERS

NEW YORK

LOUISE WAS RAISED BY A RIVER.

HER FAMILY LIVED IN A BIG HOUSE ON THE WATER
THAT WOVE LIKE A WOOL THREAD THROUGH EVERYTHING.

THE RIVER'S SOIL NURTURED A GARDEN
WHERE LOUISE AND HER FAMILY GREW
GERANIUMS, PEONIES, ASPARAGUS, AND
CHERRY TREES; APPLES AND PEARS,
PURPLE TAMARISK, PINK HAWTHORN, AND
SWEET-SMELLING HONEYSUCKLE.

ALONG ITS BANKS,
HER FATHER PLANTED POPLARS.

LOUISE KEPT DIARIES OF HER
DAYS. AND IN A CLOTH TENT
PITCHED IN THE GARDEN,
SHE AND HER SIBLINGS WOULD STAY
TILL THE DARK SURPRISED THEM,
THE LIGHT FROM THE HOUSE,
AND THE SOUND OF A VERDI OPERA,
FAR AWAY THROUGH THE TREES.

SOMETIMES, THEY'D SPEND THE NIGHT,
AND LOUISE WOULD STUDY THE
WEB OF STARS, IMAGINE HER PLACE
IN THE UNIVERSE, AND WEEP,
THEN FALL ASLEEP TO THE RHYTHMIC
ROCK AND MURMUR OF RIVER WATER.

THE RIVER PROVIDED FLOWERS AND FRUIT,
A LULLABY, AND A LIVELIHOOD.

LOUISE'S FAMILY RESTORED TAPESTRIES
— ART WOVEN FROM WOOL— AND THE WOOL
LOVED THE TANNIN-RICH WATERS,
WHICH CLEANSED AND STRENGTHENED IT,
AND ALLOWED IT TO SOAK UP COLOR.

At the family's workshop, Louise's mother, like her mother before her, repaired fabric grown threadbare with time.

She loved to work in the warm sun, her needle rising and falling beside the lilting river, perfect, delicate spiderwebs glinting with caught drops of water above her.

AND WHEN LOUISE
WAS TWELVE YEARS OLD,
SHE LEARNED THE TRADE, TOO,
DRAWING IN THE MISSING
FRAGMENTS OF A TAPESTRY.

IT WAS OFTEN THE BOTTOMS OF THESE FABRIC PICTURES
THAT GOT THE MOST WEAR
AND WERE MOST IN NEED OF REPAIR,
AND SO LOUISE BECAME ADEPT AT DRAWING FEET.
DRAWING WAS *LIKE A THREAD IN A SPIDER'S WEB.*

AMONG TAPESTRIES NEATLY STACKED LIKE BOOKS IN A LIBRARY,
LOUISE'S MOTHER TAUGHT HER DAUGHTER ABOUT FORM AND
COLOR AND THE VARIOUS STYLES OF TEXTILES.
SOME BORE ELABORATE PATTERNS; OTHERS TOLD STORIES.

SHE TAUGHT HER ABOUT THE WARP AND THE WEFT,
AND HOW TO WEAVE. THE TOOLS OF THEIR TRADE:

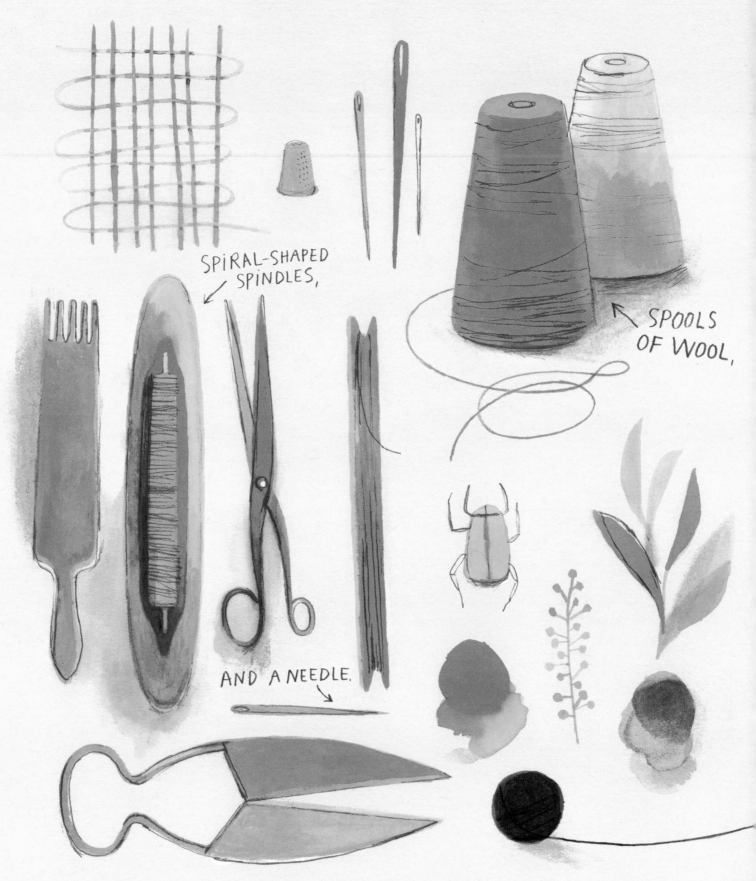

SPIRAL-SHAPED
SPINDLES,

SPOOLS
OF WOOL,

AND A NEEDLE.

SHE TAUGHT HER HOW TO DYE —
PURPLISH-RED WAS MADE FROM
CRUSHED COCHINEAL BUGS; INDIGO AND GAUDE,
OR YELLOW, FROM PLANTS;
BLACK WOOL CAME STRAIGHT
FROM THE BACKS OF BLACK
SHEEP —

AND THAT WOOL
SMELLED; THAT'S
HOW YOU KNEW
IT WAS REAL.

LOUISE'S MOTHER WAS HER BEST FRIEND.
DELIBERATE... PATIENT, SOOTHING...
SUBTLE, INDISPENSABLE... AND AS USEFUL
AS AN ARAIGNÉE (SPIDER).

LOUISE'S FATHER WAS NOT A RESTORER,
BUT HE APPRECIATED FINE THINGS.
HE BOUGHT LOUISE BEAUTIFUL
CLOTHES FROM PARISIAN
DEPARTMENT STORES.

BUT HE WAS ALWAYS LEAVING,
WHICH MADE LOUISE SO MAD,
SHE THREW HERSELF
INTO THE RIVER.

HE BROUGHT BACK CLOTH SCRAPS
FROM HIS TRAVELS, AND
LOUISE'S MOTHER FIXED THEM.

TWO HALVES OF A CLOTH
WOULD FIND THEIR WAY
BACK TOGETHER AGAIN.

*RENTRAYAGE* —
TO REWEAVE ACROSS THE CUT.

## TO MAKE WHOLE.

LOUISE FOLLOWED THE RIVER TO PARIS,
WHERE IT FLOWED INTO THE SEINE.
LITTLE DID SHE KNOW THAT ONE DAY SOON
HER BELOVED RIVER WOULD BE GONE,
FILLED IN, FLOWING NO LONGER WITH
THE WATERS THE WOOL LOVED, BUT
WITH CARS ON THEIR WAY TO THE CITY,

A MEMORY.

AT THE UNIVERSITY, SHE STUDIED MATHEMATICS. SHE LIKED SUBJECTS WITH STABILITY AND ORDER, LIKE GEOMETRY AND COSMOGRAPHY. STARS WERE PREDICTABLE. SO, TOO, THE SUNRISE, THE SETTING OF THE MOON. BUT SHE WAS DEEPLY DISAPPOINTED TO LEARN THAT MATH, LIKE LIFE, IS UNCERTAIN.

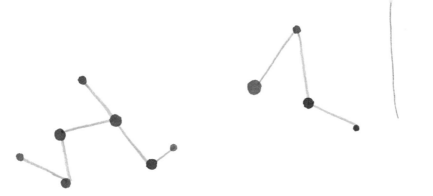

WHILE SHE WAS STILL A STUDENT, HER MOTHER
DIED. LOUISE WAS HEARTBROKEN. SHE FELT
ABANDONED AND ALL ALONE.
A THREAD, BROKEN.

SHE ABANDONED MATH
AND THE STARS AND
TURNED TO PAINTING,
APPLYING THE LESSONS
SHE'D LEARNED SO FAR
TO ART.

THE COLOR *BLUE*
*PINCHES MY HEART.*

SHE DREW,
SHE PAINTED,
SHE WOVE.
SHE MISSED HER MOTHER
SO MUCH, SHE SCULPTED
GIANT SPIDERS
MADE OF BRONZE, STEEL, AND MARBLE
SHE NAMED *MAMAN*.

HER MOTHER WAS NOT UNLIKE A SPIDER,
A REPAIRER OF BROKEN THINGS.

IF YOU BASH INTO THE WEB OF A SPIDER,
SHE DOESN'T GET MAD. SHE WEAVES AND SHE REPAIRS IT.

LOUISE GATHERED ALL THE FABRIC OF HER LIFE —

ALL THE DRESSES AND THE GARMENTS
HER FATHER HAD BOUGHT HER; ALL
THE BED LINENS, TOWELS, TABLECLOTHS,
HER NEW HUSBAND'S HANDKERCHIEFS —

AND SHE CUT IT ALL UP.

AND THEN SHE SPENT THE REST OF HER LIFE PUTTING IT BACK TOGETHER AGAIN.

SHE SEWED.

SHE STITCHED.

SHE REWORKED.

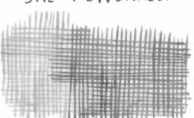

SHE WOVE.

SHE STUFFED STOCKINGS TO CREATE CLOTH SCULPTURES AND FIGURES,

A MOTHER AND DAUGHTER.

SHE SEWED COLORFUL SPIRALS AND CIRCULAR WEBS,

AND SHE SEWED SMALLER, SWEETER SPIDERS—
ONE WOVEN OF SOFT-COLORED RIBBONS,
ANOTHER OF CLOTH, DELICATE METAL.

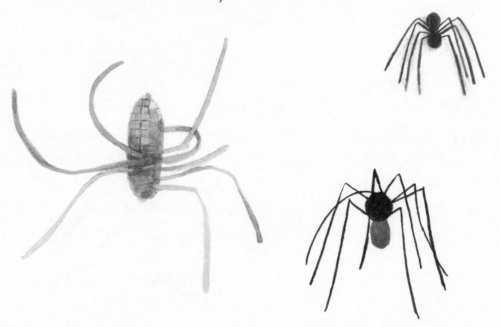

SHE MADE CLOTH DRAWINGS AND CLOTH BOOKS,
THE BLANK PAGES, NAPKINS FROM HER
WEDDING TROUSSEAU. SHE MADE BOOKS
ABOUT THE HOURS OF THE DAY AND THE DAWN,
THE RISING SUN, AND THE STARS SHE ONCE LOVED.

AND BECAUSE SHE DID NOT WANT TO FORGET
A THING, SHE MADE A BOOK ABOUT FORGETTING.

WITH THE REMAINING FABRIC OF HER LIFE,
LOUISE WOVE TOGETHER A CLOTH LULLABY.
SHE WOVE THE RIVER THAT RAISED HER —
MATERNAL PINKS, BLUES IN WATERY HUES.
SHE WOVE A MOTHER SEWING IN THE SUN,
A GIRL FALLING ASLEEP BENEATH THE STARS,
AND EVERYTHING SHE'D EVER LOVED.

WHEN SHE WAS DONE,
ALL OF HER SPIDERS BESIDE HER,
SHE HELD THE RIVER AND
LET IT ROCK HER AGAIN.

## AUTHOR'S NOTE

LOUISE JOSEPHINE BOURGEOIS WAS A WORLD-RENOWNED
ARTIST BEST KNOWN FOR HER SCULPTURES, MADE OF WOOD,
STEEL, STONE, AND CAST RUBBER, AND ESPECIALLY HER GIANT
SPIDERS, WHICH ALWAYS SEEM A LITTLE SCARY UNTIL YOU
REMEMBER THAT SPIDERS SPIN AND REPAIR WEBS; THEY ARE
WEAVERS, JUST LIKE LOUISE'S MOTHER. MAMAN, LOUISE'S
ORIGINAL SPIDER SCULPTURE, MADE OF STEEL AND MARBLE,
STANDS MORE THAN 30 FEET HIGH.

INFLUENCED BY HER FAMILY'S HISTORY OF TAPESTRY RESTORATION,
LOUISE WORKED WITH CLOTH THROUGHOUT HER CAREER, BUT IT
WASN'T UNTIL THE LAST TEN YEARS OF HER LIFE THAT
SHE BEGAN TO CREATE FABRIC DRAWINGS AND CLOTH BOOKS,
POSSIBLY AS A WAY TO COPE WITH GROWING OLDER
AS WELL AS TO CONNECT WITH MEMORIES OF HER PAST:
HER PARENTS — ESPECIALLY HER MOTHER — AND HER CHILDHOOD,
FROM WHICH SHE SAID ALL HER ART FOUND ITS INSPIRATION.

> MY CHILDHOOD HAS NEVER LOST ITS MAGIC,
> IT HAS NEVER LOST ITS MYSTERY, AND IT HAS
> NEVER LOST ITS DRAMA.

BORN ON CHRISTMAS DAY, DECEMBER 25, 1911, IN
PARIS, FRANCE, LOUISE SPENT HER CHILDHOOD IN
CHOISY-LE-ROI AND IN ANTONY, WHERE HER PARENTS
SET UP TAPESTRY-RESTORATION WORKSHOPS BESIDE
THE RIVERS. IN ADDITION TO APPRENTICING IN THE
FAMILY ATELIER, SHE STUDIED MATHEMATICS
AT THE SORBONNE. BUT WHEN HER MOTHER DIED,

LOUISE TURNED TO ART. SHE MARRIED, MOVED TO
NEW YORK, AND BECAME A MOTHER TO THREE SONS.
BECAUSE HER ART WAS NOT YET CRITICALLY ACCLAIMED,
LOUISE MADE WEAVINGS TO RAISE MONEY FOR HER
FAMILY. SHE EXHIBITED HER FIRST TAPESTRY IN 1943
AT THE AGE OF 32. SIX YEARS LATER, SHE SHOWED
HER FIRST SCULPTURES. WHEN HER FATHER DIED IN
1951, THE FAMILY TAPESTRY BUSINESS CLOSED, BUT
LOUISE CARRIED IT ON IN HER OWN UNIQUE WAY.
SHE ACQUIRED A BROOKLYN STUDIO, A FORMER GARMENT
FACTORY COMPLETE WITH SEWING MACHINES AND A

LOUISE BOURGEOIS WITH *SPIDER IV* IN 1996 (DETAIL).
PORTRAIT: ©PETER SUMNER WALTON BELLAMY / ART: © THE EASTON FOUNDATION / LICENSED BY VAGA, NEW YORK, NY

LOUISE BOURGEOIS
*SPIDER*, 2003, STEEL AND TAPESTRY, 19½ x 23½ x 25½"
PHOTO: CHRISTOPHER BURKE/ART: © THE EASTON FOUNDATION/LICENSED BY VAGA, NEW YORK, NY

SPIRAL STAIRCASE. AND AT THE AGE OF 71 SHE HAD
A RETROSPECTIVE OF HER WORK AT THE MUSEUM OF
MODERN ART, WHICH FINALLY SECURED HER PLACE
AS ONE OF THE MOST ACCOMPLISHED ARTISTS OF OUR
TIME. SHE CONTINUED TO CREATE ART UNTIL SHE DIED,
IN 2010, AT THE AGE OF 98.

QUOTES AND SOURCES

PAGE 11
[DRAWING WAS] "LIKE A THREAD IN A SPIDER'S WEB."
MORRIS, FRANCES AND MARIE-LAURE BERNADAC, EDS.
*LOUISE BOURGEOIS.* LONDON: TATE PUBLISHING, 2007.

PAGE 15
[LOUISE'S MOTHER WAS HER BEST FRIEND.] "DELIBERATE...
PATIENT, SOOTHING... SUBTLE, INDISPENSABLE... AND
AS USEFUL AS AN ARAIGNÉE." BOURGEOIS, LOUISE.
*ODE À MA MÈRE.* PARIS: LES ÉDITIONS DU SOLSTICE, 1995.

PAGE 22
[THE COLOR] "BLUE PINCHES MY HEART." COXON, ANN.
*LOUISE BOURGEOIS.* LONDON: TATE PUBLISHING, 2010
(LOUISE BOURGEOIS DIARY ENTRY, MARCH 28, 1986).

PAGE 25
"IF YOU BASH INTO THE WEB OF A SPIDER, SHE DOESN'T
GET MAD. SHE WEAVES AND SHE REPAIRS IT." COXON, ANN.
*LOUISE BOURGEOIS.* LONDON: TATE PUBLISHING, 2010
(LOUISE BOURGEOIS TAPED INTERVIEW WITH CECILIA
BLOMBERG, 1968).

PAGE 36
"MY CHILDHOOD HAS NEVER LOST ITS MAGIC,
IT HAS NEVER LOST ITS MYSTERY, AND IT HAS NEVER
LOST ITS DRAMA." BOURGEOIS, LOUISE. *ALBUM.* NEW YORK:
PETER BLUM EDITION / BLUMARTS, 1994.

TO L.B., AND TO MY *MAMAN*, BONNY.
AND TO TAMAR, FOR LOVING THIS STORY.
— A.N.

*POUR TOI MAMAN.*
— I.A.

THE ILLUSTRATIONS IN THIS BOOK WERE RENDERED
IN INK, PENCIL, PASTEL, WATERCOLOR, AND PHOTOSHOP.

LIBRARY OF CONGRESS CATALOGING-IN-PUBLICATION DATA
NOVESKY, AMY, AUTHOR.
CLOTH LULLABY: THE WOVEN LIFE OF LOUISE BOURGEOIS / BY AMY NOVESKY ;
ILLUSTRATED BY ISABELLE ARSENAULT
PAGES CM.
ISBN 978-1-4197-1881-6 (HARDCOVER)
1. BOURGEOIS, LOUISE, 1911-2010 — JUVENILE LITERATURE.
2. BOURGEOIS, LOUISE, 1911-2010 — THEMES, MOTIVES — JUVENILE LITERATURE.
I. ARSENAULT, ISABELLE, 1978– ILLUSTRATOR. II. TITLE.

N6537.B645N68 2016
730.92 — dc23
2015007769

TEXT COPYRIGHT © 2016 AMY NOVESKY
ILLUSTRATIONS COPYRIGHT © 2016 ISABELLE ARSENAULT
BOOK DESIGN BY CHAD W. BECKERMAN

LOUISE BOURGEOIS'S ART, WRITINGS, AND ARCHIVAL MATERIAL ARE
COPYRIGHT © THE EASTON FOUNDATION / LICENSED BY VAGA, NEW YORK, NY

PRINTED AND BOUND IN U.S.A.
11 10 9 8 7 6 5 4 3 2

ABRAMS BOOKS FOR YOUNG READERS ARE AVAILABLE AT SPECIAL DISCOUNTS
WHEN PURCHASED IN QUANTITY FOR PREMIUMS AND PROMOTIONS AS WELL AS
FUNDRAISING OR EDUCATIONAL USE. SPECIAL EDITIONS CAN ALSO BE CREATED TO
SPECIFICATION. FOR DETAILS, CONTACT specialsales@abramsbooks.com
OR THE ADDRESS BELOW.

THE ART OF BOOKS SINCE 1949
115 WEST 18TH STREET
NEW YORK, NY 10011
www.abramsbooks.com